HARMONIA

HARMONIA

John Moessner

STEPHEN F. AUSTIN STATE UNIVERSITY PRESS

Printed in the United States of America.

For more information:
Stephen F. Austin State University Press
P.O. Box 13007 SFA Station
Nacogdoches, Texas 75962
sfapress@sfasu.edu

Managing Editor: Kimberly Verhines
Book and Cover Design: Emily Williams
Cover Art: Ramiro Pianarosa
Author Photo: Tina Moessner

Distributed by Texas A&M Consortium
www.tamupress.com

ISBN: 978-1-62288-953-2

ACKNOWLEDGMENTS

Thanks to the editors and staff of the following publications in which these poems, sometimes in earlier versions, first appeared. *American Chordata*: "Cow on Highway." *The American Journal of Poetry*: "Angle of Repose." *American Poetry Journal*: "New Door." *Arts & Letters*: "Gravity," "Surveying the Flood." *Big Muddy*: "Memory with Fox Tails and Winter Dark," "Memory with Snowdrops and Waiting." *Canyon Voices Literary Magazine*: "Whitewood." *The Chattahoochee Review*: "If It's Too Loud." *Commonweal*: "Rodin's *Adam*," "Superposition of Grief." *The Flint Hills Review*: "A Mourning." *Free State Review*: "To the Scrap of Paper Stuck in the Retrofitted A/C Unit." *I-70 Review*: "Seam Ripper," "The Weight of It." *The Ibis Head Review*: "Ribera's *The Martyrdom of Saint Lawrence*." *Indicia*: "The Third Room." *Kestrel*: "Detective Hercule Poirot Teaches Poetry," "Sheep in Old Paintings." *Lake Effect*: "Titian's *A Monk with a Book*." *The Main Street Rag*: "The Multiple Deaths of Lennie Small." *The Midwest Quarterly*: "Controlled Burn," "Suitcase," "The Taste for Salt." *Natural Bridge*: "The Last 4th," "Mediare." *New Letters*: "Ode on an Urn." *New Ohio Review*: "Stolen Hard Drive." *The New York Quarterly*: "Spider in an Oak Tree." *Nimrod International Journal*: "Memory with Duplicate Keys and Flowers." *North American Review*: "Asleep on the Couch," "Moving." *The Opiate* (Online): "Blight," "Historic Preservation." *Plainsongs*: "Weeping Stone at 5 a.m." *Poet Lore*: "Corot's *Civita Castellana and Mount Soracte, May 1826*," "*Harmonia axyridis*." *Prairie Fire*: "Washing Hands." *River Styx*: "Attention." *Tar River Poetry*: "Blankets in a Box." *Third Wednesday*: "Sight Words." *Valparaiso Poetry Review*: "Tornado."

"Titian's *A Monk with a Book*" also appeared in the *Writers Place Yearbook 2021*.

Many thanks to Hadara Bar-Nadav for indispensable mentorship and guidance at every step of this book. Many thanks also to Jermaine Thompson and Lindsey Weishar for their friendship and insight. Thanks to Robert Stewart and Christie Hodgen for help with many of these poems. Thanks to Rebecca Morgan Frank for crucial help in the final stages of this book. Thanks also to The Writers Place, Writers for Readers, and Literacy KC. And special thanks to Michelle Boisseau, whose wisdom and example continue to instruct.

Thank you to my mother and father, Julie and Steve Moessner, for their ever-present support. Thank you to Bernice Yates and Maia Yates, who are deeply connected to the poems in this book. Thank you to Lawrence Yates, in whose memory this book is written. Lastly, my deepest thanks and love to Tina, whose readership, support, encouragement, and companionship made every part of writing this book possible.

CONTENTS

I

II

For Tina Yates

I

Suitcase

We course between two homes: one we live in,
one where your dad is dying. Three days

and our clothes spill out wrinkled and stinking,
shirtsleeves like half-gobbled worms.

Like the fish that swallowed Jonah. I was taught
he could stand, recline against the belly's wall.

Did he have a torch to light the blood-red cavern
of arched bone and oily flesh? My illustrated bible

made it more sit and wait, more contemplation,
than fish guts and bladder. I am reluctant

to unzip the suitcase's mouth, metal teeth sunk
into one another's bite, a zipped grin.

Each Friday night, we fold and slip our skins
through its unhinged jaw and pretend we aren't

travelling to Nineveh as our headlights break
on the stones of your parents' drive.

The Last 4th

The X-ray glowed, an ink-swell
like blooms bursting in a black sky.
Your cough, percussive blasts
from the black tar drum of your lungs.
Thirty years ago, you lit one, glowing
in the haze on Avenue I, your little girls
running around with sparklers shooting
from their hands, the black sky crowded
with the unfolding of hundreds of fireworks,
like an X-ray hanging far from that night.

Whitewood

Your whitewood bedframe came apart
with such ease, it seemed as if it did not feel
your weight these last twenty-four years.
You left to fetch a mallet in the basement.
It was not needed. The metal wings slid out
of their holdings like the lifting of a young weed
in soft soil. Making room for your father's hospice
bed, a chair in the corner for an overnight vigil,
we stacked each post and bar against the wall,
no longer relying on the others to stand. The date
etched in the back of the headboard not long
before you were put together, piece by piece,
each ball joint sunk gently into each socket,
as someday we each will pull apart with ease.

Titian's *A Monk with a Book*

He sits in the brown light,
fingers wrapped around a fat book

like one would hold a blunter thing,
some tool for smashing earth for umber

pigment. A labor of the mind, the gilded
boards and pages are used to mine the loam

of the brain's layers, the dry parchment
scraping the hours, searching for what,

we cannot know. God, sexual deviance,
a reason for all this silence?

Maybe he's chasing the nagging shade
that's been situated for years in his periphery,

some parable about a shrewd manager,
or the mystery of three becoming one.

The darkness of umber depends on the mix
of minerals in the soil, neither animal

nor vegetal, but other, a thing you need
to get your hands dirty to find.

Spider in an Oak Tree

A spider casts a drifting line into the openness
between two great growths of oak, backlit
by the yellow burst of a streetlamp into spokes

of light, the squeeze of wet eyes in cold wind.
The web catches the breeze, surfacing to glint
and glitter then disappear. I want to give you that

spider's legs, the sticky sureness of its lacework,
its drive to plumb the night between footing
and free fall, make you something wild-eyed, craving,

instead of the cold switch-off since your father's death.
But I can't decide if you are the spider or the caught
moth. As soon as we see an animal's grace, we see another

devour it, aspirations gone. Some nights our cast catches
the wind and grasps a woody growth in the dark,
some we are caught by a trick of thin luminescence.

I walk in the house, sweaty red, a brisk clearing
in my eyes, see the living room tangled with blankets,
bunched socks, leaves of food packaging. A small light

draws me into the bedroom to switch it off, slip
the glasses from your face. Spun with sleep,
fluid in its fabric, your splayed figure arrests me.

Angle of Repose

Of course if the material forming the flat surface becomes weak or fails, then the unsupported mass will move downward.
—Dr. Stephen Nelson, "Factors that Influence Slope Stability"

1.

You are a natural
disaster. I swim and sink in your grief. Nights
you go to sleep early, needing to rise before the sun,
enjoying the solitude of mornings, a trait you shared
with your father. Our schedules offset, no longer lovers,
but roommates in the empty house of each other's sleep.
Each footstep at night amplified, each creak
stretches and rubs against each still moment. The friction
of living bleeding into your dreams. Sometimes I wake
you and hear the babbled speech of your unconscious.
Are you okay? You are not okay. One night we sit in bed,
you want me to talk you down, or up from some depth.
I am changing from a long day of teaching.
There is a picture of your father on your dresser
where he's giving the sign for "I love you,"
meant for his deaf sister, but you hear him saying
those words each day in your head, each day
on your voicemail, and they grind against his absence.
I unbutton my shirt and toss it toward the closet,
it knocks over the frame. You snap—*Do you do that every day?*
A flash flood is deceptive, you think you see the water rising.
But there is no water, only the deep hush of an old house
waiting for the dam holding everything back to break
from my heavy footfalls. I try not to wake you.

2.

I speak about your parents'
house as if he still lives there. His watches, his car, I speak
about your father's clothes as if he still wears them.
I speak about you being your father's daughter
—*Abide with me, fast falls the eventide*—
the words from your father's funeral. I remember
the meetings, the trouble of planning a funeral
while grieving, trying to figure out songs and readings.
We were home, caught under the weight of him, caught
in the flux and movement of two large shelves of rock
pushing against each other, slipping underneath.
Caught in the unidentifiable space between tenses,
our tongues not yet adjusted to the past, his body, his death.
The cat refused food, touch, us. How do you console a grieving cat?
I remember the heft of the box they put his urn into,
buckling it into the back seat of the car during the drive
home from church. How did they get him into the urn?
Can you pour a body like liquid? Did they do it gently,
or did their hands shake with the weight of a life?
Are the properties of ash more similar to fire or stone?

Mediare

All I know is a door into the dark.
—Seamus Heaney

I've imagined my death one thousand ways:
burst star, magic trick, a lake hidden
at the bottom of a lake. Not so much what kills,

but the state immediately after. *Immediately*,
meaning *nearest in time*, *space*, *order*,
from *mediare*, *the middle*. I'll get close to it

in dreams: a gunman in an auditorium at school,
a hot muzzle pressed into my forehead, a freefall
from a fenceless bridge spanning the Royal Gorge.

Then I'll wake right before the act, my bedroom
reasserting itself in the dark, furniture shapes
hardening in my sight's bloom. Maybe death is not

the infinite other half of living, but a seam between
infinities, the quickest blink of the largest lid,
the fast inhale before submersion in water,

closing our eyes to adjust to the wetness of it all,
or feeling along the wall before the sudden
flip of lights to get our bearings in the dark.

Cow on Highway

Is this it, out here on 22, the lost cow glowing
white against the dusky sky? It could be asleep.

Drugged and drowsed by the trudging sun, I bet
it swayed heavy-lidded while grazing, chewing

the raw stalk of day. Sometimes night
offers its cold ground to hot haunches.

I, myself, feel the dead pull of rest as I center
the tractor's bucket under the bulge of its barrel.

What if my dozing were mistaken for death,
alive to the pressure from a skid's teeth

lifting my body? Why can't a tired beast lie down
to rest in the road? I look for a rise in the chest.

The Multiple Deaths of Lennie Small

1.

The first time George shot Lennie
only one person noticed. I was outside
speaking to a late student, and the rest
in the classroom had turned to their phones.
But one lonely girl, just moved to town,
gasped in the front row. She slumped
in her desk as the class scolded her
with a brief lifting of their eyes.
The shot echoed off the cold green tiles
of the walls, the A/C box wet
with condensation. Slow beads
of cooled vapor streaked to the floor.

2.

The second time George shot Lennie I watched.
My whole class, not a child gone, jumped
at the scene, their attention not ready
for the crashing prop gun blast that reverberated
throughout the forest on screen. The diffuse light
saturated everything as the music faded in.
I turned down the volume and snapped
on the lights. The room lit up with the debris
of movie snacks that had accumulated in the aisles.
That classroom had never been more silent.
Silence has its own long memory of the world:
a school in summer with freshly waxed floors,
the cold stillness of a radiator over winter break,
the abrupt absence in a body's limp form, broken
by the sound of the bell shooting through the halls.

3.

Sometimes at night
I will see the same thirty seconds of an event
like a continuous reel playing back a crucial moment
until I see what I hadn't seen before: two boys fighting
in my third hour, their red faces, sweaty foreheads,
the impossible tightness of their small shaking fists.
This time I noticed the weight of the gun,
the tiny quiver in his voice dipping like a hand
tired from gripping a pistol, tired of making a fist.
The third time George shot Lennie the sun had risen
high enough to haze the image on the screen,
the dust on the outside of the windows blanking everything.
The whole room looked like a washout, what editors
use to signify the afterlife, or a dream, leaving it
for the audience to decide.

4.

Lennie did not immediately die the fourth time
George raised the gun to his head. The fire alarm
sounded before he could pull the trigger. I paused
the movie and herded my students into the late-May heat.
Lennie was left sitting in the forest, the sound of water
close by, the settled feel of pressed grass and leaves,
the dapple and shine of sunlight through trees.
He could talk about rabbits forever. But poor George,
holding the gun, potential energy burning in his hand,
rising with each paused second. No one in the room
to witness, just him and Lennie looking for a final peace.
But he couldn't pull the trigger. Not even the strength
of Lennie's own hand could throw the hammer.
Lennie hadn't said his line. It was so nice outside,
the breeze blowing dandelion seeds across the field.
We all need a break from the relentless march of day
to watch clouds drift, feel the grass bend under our weight,
watch it spring up slowly after we've gone.

5.

The last time George shot Lennie
my students called it a kindness,
they called it mercy. I asked them
if Lennie seemed happy at the end
looking out over a stream, seeing rabbits
dance around in his head. I asked
how they felt about George
being the one to do it, calming Lennie
by telling him about a life he hoped
soon to be a part of. They asked me
what I thought about the afterlife,
if I believed in God. Maybe God
comes to us in many forms, like happiness,
a giant rabbit, the voice of a friend
gripping a gun. I told my students
I don't know what comes after death,
but I hope it's as nice as what Lennie saw.
A student reminded me Lennie wasn't real,
that it was just a movie made from a book,
and I realized how hard you have to work
to be happy, how no one can teach you that.

Attention

Before she forgot who I was, Grandma Kathleen
told me about a button on my brow
that could take away my anger. I was six,

cradled in her blue-veined arms, steaming
from my brother's cruel joke. I don't remember
what he did, but in her brick front room

she pressed her thumb between my eyes
and dimpled its pad into my smooth skin.
My ear to her chest, she whispered a spell.

My mind was flustered by the mysteries of touch,
by the gentle attention of her curved thumb,
like a door, suddenly there, opened.

The Weight of It

Even the slightest test of its heft, a timid lift
to get a feel for it, leaves me a beetle up against

God, or the leftover scraps from God's binging
dinner. Curved like the run of a dry, creamy bone,

the rib of some extinct animal dropped
from the canopy. I will piecemeal it apart.

A small ten-inch saw, teeth no bigger
than a raindrop. The guy-wire is taut

and twangs with each cross-section pull.
Each appendage, each jutting line of wood

and capillary, gives me a sense for life
among grass blades, the repeated beauty

of smaller and smaller terms: trunk, bough, limb,
stick, twig, sawdust. The dead weight of it all.

The Taste for Salt

I know that you are hungry and you are tired,
and that you are tired for being hungry,

that your hunger dwells in equal measure, in equal appetite
as your exhaustion, and that the two play off each other

as sequential parts of a song that when sung suggest
the other as its completion, and they continue in that round

supporting and countering through endless rehearsals
of some terrible concert for which you are preparing.

I know that your hunger no longer resembles the taste for salt,
or the excitement for raspberry jam and honey on bread,

the full gulp of a glass of milk, but manifests now as an ache
for an absence of pain. But I also know that today

we saw the pointed form of a dog shoot straight
in the twilight to howl, and we looked up in expectation

of something howling in us, anything to evoke an action
equal to that dog's devotion, and in not seeing the sky,

we saw instead the lacing of oaks covering the path,
and you said I wish I could float parallel to the ground

and see the canopy scroll above me, that you wanted it
to be your final wish before you die, and in that silence the wind

came into the still-green oak leaves and I said it was beautiful,
and you said this is enough to count this world as good.

Harmonia axyridis

The curved shell of an Asian lady beetle, bleached
white, bent the afternoon light around itself on the sill,
its spots the color of dried blood on an old shroud.

A quiet porcelain grave, it still maintained a gloss
like the glaze of an ancient urn, thrown,
then fired in the early Southern sun. It died

looking out onto the wild vines that flexed the chain-link
fence of our backyard, like an old woman asking
to move her bed so she could look out the window.

Rodin's *Adam*

> *...the tragic pleasure of admiration.*
> —Auguste Rodin

He stumbles from that stone womb
with rocky sleep in his eyes, still
a curl in the toes. He is cast in the first
morning's bronze light. The fig tree's wild
beauty, the grass's strange softness, sharp
contrast from the rock his foot is anchored to.
Rodin captured the spastic flex in the unfolding,
the softening of metallic lines into the run
of the calf, the blooming tufts of hair.
He's the best and the worst of us. The first
to feel alone, the first to cast blame, the last
to know the light of eternal day. His eyes
contain both the blank gaze and the shadow
from his brow furrowed in ugly confusion.
The knowing finger points down. Hiding
in the clay, there is always something
holding us back, a catch in the breath,
the muscles never relax.

Blight

runs a block dry, cut off
like a limb without blood, clots

stuck like leaves in chain-link.
I pass DJ's Snack Shack on my way

to the downtown library. Closed
for the day, year, generation, a sign hangs

perpendicular to the fading facade,
once white, now baked to the color

of creamed corn advertised in the window.
The next block over, on Cherry Hill,

lawns choke on thistle, crabgrass, thorny
brush, home to the fauna of wild systems.

You remind me of this town, your sorrow
a kind of blight, growing over your smile,

weakening the hiccup of your laugh,
like blood avoids that part of town.

Sight Words

I have two eyes, she said, her pace slow,
her tongue cradling each syllable, turning

them around mid-word to fit the keyhole
of her memory, inching forward like a boat

against the current. *I have two eyes* rang again
from the slow bell of her mouth.

She looked up from the exercise, peering through me
to the projection of the phrase in her mind.

Every Tuesday was the first Tuesday we met, her stroke
leaving her unable to remember the phrases on the page,

a net to carry water. I mouthed it slowly, her eyes fixed
on my lips, squinting into the dark-red cavern of my mouth.

She shook her head. I saw her say it a week ago
and almost cried at her success. The words were locked

behind a door in the dark, a black hole of language
and phrase, or resting at the bottom of a lake filling

from a swollen stream. Water welled in her eyes,
she shut them before looking down to greet the syllables

again for the first time. Surfacing, she tried it
without looking, but it vanished like water falling

through her cupped hands before reaching her lips.

The Third Room

Not knowing what to do with the extra room,
we opened the shades and gave it to the sun.
The dust whirled around in the warmed air.

First, we left the door open, glancing
at the oddity of space, amazed at the feeling
of emptiness, the bare hush, the light's rays

sifting and sighing through the window's
wrinkled glass. But one day the door was shut.
Neither of us would admit to closing it.

The growing pressure glared in the sun
as a fine film of dust covered the floor,
settling at the lowest point.

Asleep on the Couch

You were often too sad to have sex.
It was a terrible year: the anxiety
of the audit at work, the break-in
just before spring, your father dying.
Each meal sat like stones on your plate
or pebbles in your stomach.
Sleep bled into sleep like the flicker
of the TV into the dark hallway
you no longer walked down, choosing
instead to remain on the couch,
settled into simultaneous states
of conscious and unconscious grief.
I studied your topography laid out
in the living room, the muted TV's glow
and its shadows blanketing you.
I wanted to sop your scent with my lips,
feel the free weight of your red hair
on my shoulders, measure you to find
what you lost. I wanted you to want it,
to want me. Instead, I sat on the edge
and held your hand, cupped it like a lost
ladybug. I urged you to move to the bed
for the night, knowing it would be better
to wake up somewhere else.

To the Scrap of Paper Stuck in the Retrofitted A/C Unit:

It will soon be over. There is only so much space between
the float and the crash, and eventually you will be fished out

and tossed into the trash, ending your mad flailing against the wind.
But even in the expanse of sky above the football field,

it would only take a body a few minutes to drop from an airplane
crisscrossing the cyan, a small sliver of Earth's atmosphere, where

I am told the whole is thinner than the skin of the unfinished apple
bruising itself on a stack of papers on my desk. How many of us

haven't stared out of a classroom window wishing we were flying
at 35,000 feet, or feeling the dip in the stomach from free fall

off the local high dive, instead of finishing a black board assignment?
Today it's a final letter to their future selves, five years from now,

an envelope addressed to be sent somewhere. Some make it, some don't.
The morning started out hot and by the time the afternoon sun hit

my wall of windows above the A/C unit, the room was ready to burst,
students crowding the chipped wooden door, the air blowing, warm,

loud with the sound of thirty seniors ready to go out and find someone
else to tell them what to do. And when you were torn from the edge

of a task before it was turned into a pedestal for half-eaten apples,
did you think you'd float above the air vent and feel the rush?

The bell rings and only a few students turn to wave goodbye
before streaming out, a river of arms and backpacks.

They fly down the halls and into the humid haze of summer break,
exploding off the buses, drifting to parks, the local pool, unburdening

of a year's worth of paper and books, no longer practicing math, or fire alarms,
or lock downs. Sometimes we get stuck between the ripping liftoff

and the flipping fall, jammed into a space, stalled, forgetting how it feels
to stop drifting, waiting for someone to turn off the wind. I am almost out

the door when a student returns to hand me their assignment. I add it to the rest:
future artists, doctors, athletes, the occasional teacher, it's the same every year.

Detective Hercule Poirot Teaches Poetry

Poirot teaches Hastings that everything is important,
every detail. Even the least in the smallest hour speaks:
the tea in the cup, the half-eaten meal before bed,

the powder on the tray outside her room. So many clues hide
in the scattering of life's artifacts, ordinary monuments
like water glasses and crumb-sprinkled plates, museum pieces

plumbing purpose and plot. Finger smudges on the computer,
umber drips of coffee splattered across the counter,
book stacks placed in temporary spots on the seats of chairs.

Of these I know little, and say little for fear of interrupting them.
But I cannot shake the lust for knowledge, to know what paths
were taken at 18 to find my wife in choir class, which day

brought the breeze that planted the linden at my window,
what passing through death's heavy velvet feels like, and if
I will have to paw at the folds to find the split. The silence

after my questions ties me into a knot of more questions.
Poirot sits examining the room, and I read as the murder unfolds
on the fibrous, yellowed pages. Whose hands have thumbed,

folded, bent these two book halves on a wide-open afternoon
like this? The quality of light drawing itself through the blinds
hushes me. It's the same light that pours through the waving glass

of a third-floor study onto a muddy boot print on a Persian rug.
Poirot instructs Hastings to recount the events of the previous night,
each thing as it was, as it continues to be. When did the brief rain settle

the dust of a hazy evening, how long was the window open?
The mind frantically flips to the next page where Hastings, bathed
in the light that often signals understanding, is dumbfounded.

Moving

...what makes anything poignant is that it's going to end.
—Michelle Boisseau

Zeno's paradox says you never actually arrive,
never make it to the hands-on-knees moment
where you unshoulder all that kept you moving
through the sour and sweat of task after task,
each a half-length beyond. I'm packing boxes
of pens and ramekins and books and lightbulbs,
like Sisyphus on the mountain planting a heel
into a well-worn groove the shape of his foot.
I imagine after some time, three weeks, 100 years,
he would have wished he believed in Zeno's trick,
would have preferred the constant grunt and goal
of one singular task never grasped to the eternal
cliff after each achievement. I can't remember
how many times I swept the wood floors
with the blue-bristled broom, how many stoops
to catch the piles with the black dustpan.
Our universe is expanding. Some say it will one day
contract, gravity the brush that moves in concentric
circles around the room to drag balls of dirt and dust
to the center, or like the collapsing of plates
and bowls into a box, only to expand again
into cupboards and cabinets of a new home.
Each house lulls me into the safety of permanence,
the full settle of a body on a mattress. Still,
I find myself cleaning baseboards and ordering a truck.
Once, I mopped myself into a corner, losing track

of my exit, dividing the room by halves until
I was squared into the last dry unpolished patch.
Hours could have passed, or minutes under water,
but I feel I lived a lifetime there, my soles running
with the woodgrain, my breath rising into its own
echo. I watched wet nebulae disappear on the floor
until it looked just like it did when we moved in.

Blankets in a Box

Folds of cotton sewn onto layers of fleece,
rough wool and a fringe of intertwined tassels,

a square yard of alpaca, all of these bulging
in a cardboard box stacked in a truck trailer,

colors gone dark in the long night of a closed lid.
One traveler, a springy brown stink bug, crawls

through layers of tucked ceilings and floors. How best
does one illustrate the plane of being to a bug?

It could have had a whole house to flutter through,
an empty pleasure tomb to trace, to ponder an insect's

extent. Instead, it fell into the static threads, the deep pile
of warm winter. How soft its loneliness, how quiet,

so close to the woven framework it roams? The muffled
world of rattling trailer panels, of jacked axels, hardly

penetrates to the center, a second womb, egg sack, time
as obscure as direction, and as close as the future folded

over its knobby back. Unaware of the miles and a hundred
boxed worlds, it could have fallen into the vertical

craning of lamps, the corded coiling of power cables.
Dumped on the floor, an echo unfolding through

an empty room, it met with an eternity of wood grain,
a diffuse brightness pouring in through the walls.

Memory with Duplicate Keys and Flowers

I keep seeing the clerk as he stands, bracing
his waist against the sun-faded counter, bent
over the key duplicator cutting new teeth
into the metal tongue of a key blank. Following
the rise of each ridge, the slip of each notch,
he turns the stylus to guide the cutting edge
down the keyway of a copy, twinned
turnings like entangled particles, or nothing
like them at all

like the flowers that bloomed
the spring we moved here, our tongues
tracing their petaled names: bloodroot,
bluebell, phlox, floss flower. Each one
like a spoken copy of the flower's ridges,
each dip into the cup collecting rain, copies
made in warm breath floating to unlock
some newness in each other's ears, a turning
of seasons, a final thaw from the frozen
brokenness of our year

like a bad peach
unwilling to give up its pit, the fruit hard
and unyielding. I can't remember what keys
he was making, our new home, the couple
who moved in after, the splintered jamb
with the deadbolt thrown like an anxious
hand reaching out to helpless air. Each key
has two parts: its brazen body and the negative
housing it slips into, a peach pit clinging
to fibrous flesh, your name blooming
in the cradle of my open mouth, grief
and the mind it opens like a picked lock.

Angle of Repose

The forces resisting movement down the slope are grouped
under the term shear strength which includes frictional resistance
and cohesion among the particles that make up the object.
— Dr. Stephen Nelson, "Factors that Influence Slope Stability"

3.

The foothill is not finished
forming, the loose boulders and scree fall prey to gravity,
each loss contributes to its shape over a lifetime.
We walked along a path in Arkansas and saw the hanging shelves
of rock walls, hidden streams dripping, licking the stones
with their secret wet mouths. The trees had been changing
for a month. It was four months since your father passed.
You wept in the quiet car ride, three hours from Kansas City.
An underground stream finds daylight and emerges.
Does water evaporate underground?
There were slow cool drafts through the underside of the cliff.
It's been months since we first learned the diagnosis
—the slow boil of hard stone—gravity pulled
a tree down across the path in front of us,
we stepped over the bulge of its trunk. Wet moss,
damp wood, hundreds of bugs seething under the bark,
in the rotted-out places blackened by mold and lack.
The trip was a chance for rest. We stopped moving
as a deer passed through the brush ahead,
yards between us, and silence. We are still learning
how to be married, to catch falling debris.
Grief, like rain, like an underground stream pulling
at the roots and weakening the bedrock. You wiped

your face as we walked. The long sleeves of my flannel
dangled off your thin arms. A dam at the end
of the trail, you arrived first, stunned, a whole lake
waiting to break through. I reached you
out of breath. We hadn't spoken for an hour.

4.

We started climbing
through a field of larkspur and columbine.
You wanted to lay down and sink into the flora,
become the soil caught by the weave of roots,
become a thing singular and many.
We crossed a creek, its nameless purity
surfaced in the valley from under the mountain.
An entrance to a mine marked the mountain's grief,
cancer of the West. It was more rounded mass
than romantic peak, two great plates of earth
jamming themselves into each other's arms.
We left the valley's flowers and climbed up
loose plates of rock like shattered pottery. Our missteps
sent showers of falling rubble down the slope.
The sun reigned the blue sky and we reached
the top where we could look out across the valley.
You reached into your bulging pack, your hand stained
as you pulled out a smashed container of bright
red raspberries, seedy wet pulp, their color popping
against the gray of the ground. You licked your fingers
and offered me a smashed pinch as it started to snow,
tiny flat flakes like ash from a great fire burning above us.
It was all so gray, the snow, the creek below, the valley
of flowers, out of focus, miles away. We hiked down,
a mountain's worth of climbing squeezing the juice
from our bodies. The stream in the valley ran louder,
the flowers gained their color, the mountain grew
small behind us.

5.

The Fourth of July, 2016,
We played badminton out front of your house.
Your father complained about the fireworks
exploding near his window. He sat waiting for sleep,
and the inevitable waking two hours after. Your mother
declined three invitations to join the block party.
Didn't they know she was walking on tiptoe around
the short fuse of his temper? Your mother nursed him
to small levels of comfort, an extra pillow, a handful
of pills, cleaning piss off the toilet, never more
than a room away. The cancer reached his frontal lobe,
traveling up the highway of pumped blood from his lungs.
Amateur flashes of red and blue, bright veins of flame
from an exploding heart, the ash and debris snuffing
out on the lawn. Your father wanted a hotel for the night.
We are getting a room, it wouldn't be cheap, *I won't sleep here*,
the fireworks would stop soon, *why aren't we leaving yet?*
A sleepless night spent at the hotel watching TV.
Only a slight drifting off, then up at three, waiting to go
back home to the plush loveseat propped up on risers,
littered with magazines and medical supplies.
The slow movement of a hurricane taunts
the connotations of emergency. Plenty of time
to prepare, to gather belongings. Plenty of time
to say goodbye. There is no time left.
This is not the man she married.

Corot's *Civita Castellana and Mount Soracte, May 1826*

Two windows in my room: the neighbor's garden,
with their tomato plants drooping in the sun, a pile of soil

in the corner ready for a spade, a discarded denim shirt
lying in the shade, and in the other a picture of a mountain,

not the largest item in the frame, but defined and detailed,
like meeting someone's eyes across a field. In both of these

there is the sky, the largest thing in either viewpoint, punching
through gaps in trees, brimming the ridge of a minor peak,

yet disregarded, a background to show perspective and distance.
I assume Corot laid the boundaries of blue and white,

giving the canvas time to dry before setting down the mountain
and its skirt of trees and buildings and the brown hazy ground.

The order is reversed in the other. The earth collected first,
then plants birthed from the waters to prepare the sky to be

consumed, so delicious with its varied blues. For me, stuck
in this afternoon room, numb to the fan's currents, the backdrop

of its droning, this is the only thought: Being so connected
to the landscape, brush over brush, stacking canvasses like days,

I wonder if Corot noticed this reversal of order, the shifting
dominance of focus. That in order to understand this world,

sometimes you need to reverse engineer it, put it back together
with your own hands, or at least imagine what that would feel like.

II

Tornado

The crowd billowed into the entryway, mingling
in the low pressure of a midtown lunch break,
coats gray as the clouds piling up above the restaurant.

The rumble of voices was cut by the tornado siren.
Customers crouched in the walk-in, under tables,
the bathroom stalls, everyone hugging interior walls,

the floor wet with rainwater from their shoes.
A line cook, hearing the slice of siren sharpen itself
along the electric air, grabbed a kitchen knife

and ran outside, pushing against a swarming front
of bodies rushing for cover. Deliberate as a freight train,
she chanted some words of protection and slashed

the air, her voice coming and going in fierce breaths,
spun prayers thrown at the sky, becoming wind.

Memory with Fox Tails and Winter Dark

A trailing of foxes or the wormy nakedness
of searching opossums, it was hard to tell in the stark
canvas of winter stretching over central Missouri
as the train snaked along the bending track toward
our reluctant new home. Like a spine at rest on a mattress
or water finding the curve of a drain, the gentle sweep
of tails following swift bodies, this small pack of low
snouts crouched along a ditch slope lining a stand of trees,
hugging the brief hill before the deep cover of pine swept
their faint figures from the slate of night

like fitful dreams

during the first sleep in our new house, its cold dimensions
catching me in a panic as I woke with the rattle of a drafty
window. Wide-eyed and thirsty for familiar shapes, I looked
out and thought I saw those same figures disappear
foraging for trash behind a detached garage, their shadows
pouring into the pool of night brimming the streetlight
bleeding into the whispered rise of morning, the small
lamp of daybreak come to soften me like snow melt.

If It's Too Loud

I like the hidden glitter of an old amp's grill cloth,
the glint of the dented drip edge, and the turn-on,
eye-like, of the power indicator, it's flick and jiggle
as the bulb loses its tight socket grip. I like the drip

of sweat down the channel of the back, a body caught
in the crowd, a current of arms. I like the slap-
back echo of wet, twangy notes through the rusted spring
of a reverb tank, their return off speckled club walls,

the rattle in the metal of my garage roof. I like the dazzle
and doom of the drum kit, chrome smudged by sure,
calloused hands, the sparkle of the cans matted by dust
from a long stint in a basement. I like it all, the sore shoulders,

throbbing heels, even the hearing loss, now a high-pitched ring
from years of lost ear plugs, like a dripping faucet, loudest
in the quiet of an early-to-bed Saturday night, pushing
like an elbow in the back, louder, louder, louder.

Controlled Burn

Bluestem, switchgrass, coneflower, a seam of fire
rips across a field like the ring eating

a smoldering cigarette. There are always fires
burning. A whip of caramel stings the nostrils, a bite

on the tongue, second-hand singe. The prairie retreats
inward to survive the fire's steady effacement,

a glowing snake molting skin of thin ash.
Inhale, slow burn, the snubbed stalks above

cough dead growth to the hot air, and afterwards,
breathless, stones and creek beds pop

against the charred landscape, like bones,
a black map of what remains.

Ribera's *The Martyrdom of Saint Lawrence*

for Lawrence Yates

Black wood and blacker smoke, the fullness
of bearded men and a woman mourning beneath
ash and a cloak cut from oxen hide, through
all this, Lawrence's face shines like the fire's
heart, his palms darkened by charred ground.
We lingered, speechless, in front of this scene,
letting our wives go on to the next gallery.
This was six months before we knew about your body,
how tar had taken root in your lungs.
How could you breathe with those thick masses,
like felted wool or thunderheads? We saw Lawrence,
gasping for room to breathe, drawn into the carbon
cloud to burn. But, first, the supplication,
opening wide his bright chest.

Gravity

rounds everything, the path of Earth,
the Moon's muted body, a tongue
of water off a sheer cliff, the arc
of a shuttlecock, feathers raking the air,
falling slowly, and dying suddenly
an inch in front of your outstretched racket.
We played on a hot, humid evening
in July when the Sun made its movements
noticeable and sure. Your father was in bed
trying to sleep while the world exploded
with extra hours of daylight. Your mother
shut the drapes, as if to stop the Sun
from reminding him that, while his head
was darker and full of the black sink
of sickness, there was still a star
devoted to the living, letting us believe
it's the one falling, that we are the center
of its dance, like you have fallen into
my arms at night, the small attraction
of my consolation, a planet pulling slightly
on its star. But really, it is us who fall,
fell, will fall, poured like a body into
the outstretched arms of a lover.

Angle of Repose

But for the moment everything's an ache
Deferred, foreknown, imagined and most real.
—Seamus Heaney

6.

You traveled home
the day he died. You were heading to give your mother
a break, miles of asphalt snaked between our two houses
measuring the distance between childhood and adulthood.
He was in a hospice room lying in bed, a room he walked into
of his own volition. The pain started, and the requests.
I know they have the drugs, please, just let me end it.
Your mother told him that was illegal, *I don't care,*
the nurses know where the drugs are. His legs swelled
with neglect, purple and smooth, his skin taut
and blotchy, no longer hiding the blue tangle
of his veins. They gave him enough drugs to slip
into unresponsiveness. His body convulsed
with the respirator.

7.

Vermont, our honeymoon,
two years before his death. We decided to climb Mount Abraham
and set off through the forested growth of the Green Mountains.
It was wet and lush, like walking into the yawning mouth
of a tree. We could feel the water in the air as our legs burned.
We reached the end of the forest and scrambled over
smooth rock. The top was bald and exposed.
You wish I liked to hike more, but I did not enjoy it.
On our way down, we watched tree trunks pass by
and were caught off guard by a small stream.
There was no stream on the way up. We continued down, lost.
My legs burned with panic. The sun was setting
and droplets of water pinged the arching arms of pine trees.
They danced and waved. You thought it was beautiful.
I admired your calm. An hour passed like wind through the trees,
the absence of any other noise but my heavy breathing.
We will remember this for the rest of our lives.

8.

February, seven months
since he died. I was teaching at the university.
I came home at noon to find the door kicked in, splinters
of jamb and the Christmas wreath littered
the entryway, along with clothes from our dresser
and a busted lamp left behind in the rushed exit.
The key still outstretched in my shaking hand,
I backpedaled to the porch and waited for the police.
The full weight of loss takes time to sink in.
The TV, computer, watches, jewelry, my clothes.
I imagine them slipping a shirt over their heads,
feeling the body of fabric open up and settle onto their torsos,
finding it wanting, or perfect with pre-worn give.
They stole the hard drive your dad gave you filled
with home movies. The Christmas before he died, we watched
them at your parents' house. You curled up on the couch
you slept on in high school when you were sick. Your dad
would get up at 3 a.m. and move your stubborn sleep-self to bed.
You were addicted to it, the crying, laughing, snot.
In a world where it is difficult to be happy, sadness offers a kind
of grounding, lets you know yourself, how deep the water is,
and how far you have to swim to surface.

9.

Breath leaves the body
every moment and comes back with numbing regularity.
Even the pump and spit of a respirator fades into the background
of a conversation between family. Only when it stops
do we look up and see death has swept by and stolen it away.
After a minute of watching, we realize it is gone forever,
the chest stuck in permanent exhale with no more room for air.
Sitting at the foot of the bed while sisters, aunts, a wife
paused, I saw you walk into the room, having missed
what we all missed: the last moment, the last echo
of the last rock, and the quiet of the rest of a life. The foothill
is not finished forming. You keep losing and sloughing off
memories of him, that year, the years before months before the end.
A picture with a new frame, or no frame at all, you continue
to scan your past until you notice what's missing, or what wasn't
there all along. The foothill isn't finished forming.
We won't know the shape of grief, or the shape of a life,
until the last rock slips. Then, some underground stream finds
its mouth, and starts singing in the daylight, along with life
crawling out of every crack, the cave that is left behind.

Stolen Hard Drive

It contained home movies where he wore
goggle-sized glasses, a toweled shoulder holding
a small redhead at a birthday party, three hours

of ripped paper like static on a radio, the sun
flaring off the ripples of the neighborhood pool.
What do those thieves think of your soccer games,

the *Go girl!* and the rain that drove him cursing to the car?
What about last Christmas? He was too tired, so you held
the camera instead and closed in on his drooped head

nodding while everyone opened gifts. Would they tear up
thinking of their fathers, would it convince them to call more?
Ripped from your life, just a plastic box in a bag of stuff.

Maybe before wiping it clean, they will browse your home
movies, say, *What a good father, what a good life.*

Superposition of Grief

Your father is stuck in the past, an oxbow lake
left behind in the curve of time's waste. Your grief
is anchored to his death, a line of memories unspooling
behind you as you drift forward in the river's searching.

Like water tipped from a cup carried to bed, or the splash
on the bathroom tile from a too-full tub, it is hard to gather
your sadness without spilling more of it, a measure
of a body bound only by the negative space it brims.

Each day is a new attempt to survey grief's coursing,
each food-triggered memory, each line of music heard
in his nobody's-watching voice. And it's impossible to tell
which life supplies your sorrow, his rigored past, or his future,

evaporated. You're living every day in new depths,
each waking a plumb line fed into the dark body
surrounding you. But to see how deep the river really runs,
you will need to be something other than the river.

Caravaggio's *Saint John the Baptist in the Wilderness*

Surrounded by wilderness, dark foliage,
floppy flora at his feet, the grizzled growth

of hedge and branch, some glow in his radiance,
communing with the blood-red folds of his shawl

that spill over his modest form, but mostly they breathe
in dim obscurity, half-known shapes lurking

behind this strange visitor, so sad and forlorn.
Do they feel the temptation to toss his hair

with a tendril, run a shooting stem along the arch
of his foot? Or do they wish him gone,

the space his body illuminated expanding again
into the close and quiet worship of the dark?

Seam Ripper

Split-tongued and sweeping
valley of mouth, all sharp edges,

the pull-through cuts each stitch,
each woven cord. Sink the teeth

into the cross-stitch, the blanket,
the broken chain, even the lazy daisy,

pulling taut, then sliding clean along
the silver knife of the body, the bound,

the sutured, trees of threads reaching
into the space between us, hands

falling from each other's grip. Run
yourself along the edge of grief,

sever before you mend.

Surveying the Flood

Pelicans lifting from tree limbs and irrigation pumps surrounded by water,
the sky giving a squinted brightness off the water,
not a single point of light, but a surrounding diffusion, like water
vapor, like it isn't really there, like this water
isn't supposed to be here, at least not this much water.
This valley used to be all water,
a body of salt and weed, a sea
dividing this land as continents drifted on plates of molten rock like water,
and some continents trailed others to cut off the ocean
from itself, much like this water
cuts off fields from fields, segments the highway that snakes through the
   chain of lakes,
like a single string transformed into a draping of gems, each a different pool
of light decorating the valley's neck, lapis lazuli, topaz, sapphire, the sun
   flashing off the waves
like silver seed heads of grain after it rains.

Weeping Stone at 5 a.m.

The basement flooded again.
I woke with the storm and shuffled
down to watch the water weep

through limestone and cement.
You were already up
clearing the drain

in the driveway, the water
pulling leaves and mud
into the iron grate.

Rain lashed at your clothes,
dripping from the bends
in your joints, the bottom

of your pajama pants,
and you sulked inside,
wet as a lost cat. I heard

your sloppy footsteps
on the wooden floors above.
You came downstairs and we laid

towels on the floor. You said
Water finds its way into anything.

Washing Hands

They washed your father's body before they burned it,
the sopping sponge, the detail of practiced work, the way
only a wet hand can fit the shape of skin. I learned

at a young age to love the calmness, the coolness
of washing my hands, the folded repetition, a prayer
to cleanliness and order. Sometimes I let the tap's mouth run

over my palms, grace my wrists, let them be kissed,
a sacrament of ordinary devotion, like a father washing
his daughter's hands while she stands on a stool.

Instead of living on a river, we brought the river to us.
Maybe it's the sound of a faucet flipped open, the instinctual
trickle in the ear, life banking through a dense wood.

So returns the faint memory, our past selves wandering,
tongues dry as our dusty hair, the thick leather of our hands
hardened like amphora in a kiln. I like to think they practiced

on every other body before washing his, learning each
curve, following the lines of limbs to their source,
the spots where life builds up. Time rounds out a body

like a stone in a stream. One last touch of the river's dripping
lips, before turning back into earth, dry, waterless.

Ode on an Urn

When old age shall this generation waste,
Thou shalt remain, in midst of other woe
–John Keats

Rounded, like a bent knee, and smooth,
like the matte feel of a room lit through
opaque glass. The geometry of something
shaped by hands, its curves always return
to itself. A body for a body, or a collection

of the body's elements: fire, sand, bone, earth.
Time is still underneath its closed lid, a fixed point,
a dark cavity, quiet, except for the dull
echo of the world outside, turning, turning
always forward toward some bright, fiery end.

Historic Preservation

The walls of a 19th-century church are cracking
and falling away, and you try to save them.
The stained glass is brittle. The shallow panes
darkened by damp and smoke from fires.

The mortar looks jammed and fudged,
used as a stopgap to fill holes, nests
of spider silk. Your father bragged through
his raspy speech that you were saving history,

the prayers and songs of so many, his spit thick
as lime, the branches of his lungs smeared
with cancer's weighty pull. You hear the sound
of stones crumbling away and the gritted pass

of the trowel, the last breaths of a man surrounded
by women singing, sobbing, quiet as ash.

New Door

I want the old door back, the 10,000-day door, its snug fit opening
faithfully and gently, its ease taken for granted like a valve

of the heart ushering us through to a body of rooms. I approach
the landing each day with my key outstretched and return to a door

slightly open, still like a broken limb. It kept the world out
until it could no longer brace against the boot of a thief.

How many blows until it buckled, wooden shards like loose teeth?
I hope they noted the smell of our home, found it as inviting

as our absence. New door, what can you give except this toxic scent
permeating the entryway? We unlock the memory of that day

every time we key you and put a shoulder to your stuck state.

A Mourning

You float on a rimless sea
in a boat too big for you, where once
a man rowed and sang so quietly
you strained to hear his voice.
But that voice is lost. You sharpen
your eyes against the dark and try
to make a choice in a sea of infinite
choices, a stroke forward, a stroke back,
no markers to measure progress of a future
lost. An endless dream picking up
where you left off night after night.
How can I listen in the early morning,
calm your sobbing, look you in the eyes,
unless I, too, have drifted on that sea?
Forgive me if I refuse to tell you
everything will be all right.

Sheep in Old Paintings

After the paintings of Claude Gellée, called Le Lorrain
at The Nelson-Atkins Museum of Art

They are doing the day's work, sniffing
and chewing, heads down to rummage
the earth's shoots and tubers, a universe
expanding with each inspection.
A bit fat, but their postures indicate
steady motion, hoofs following snouts.

Do they regard the shepherd and his piping?
He's no use since they've been stuck
in the same glen for 400 years. Do they hear
the slipped notes, the languor in his trills,
the trailing off at the end of each tune
in the sweat and haze of the singular afternoon

hung on the horizon? Framed with contrast
and classical balance, do they long for the green
on distant slopes, water misting at the river's edge,
or have they been driven mad by the tyranny
of perfection's endless season? I bet it's all old
to them after centuries, champing the same patch

of Campagna, the stretched gradient of sky,
the storm of foliage bursting on every tree,
the worn-out folkish songs. Even the spectators
gazing in would be as common as clover,
those bored eyes that see yet another minor work,
or those who yearn to feel the breeze through

the Roman countryside and lean in to spy another
sheep hidden in the dark growth of brushwork
at the thicket's edge. I imagine nothing is miraculous
to these sheep after 400 years of twilight and hunger
gnawing their guts, nothing, except their eternal grazing,
the timeless bounty blooming under their muzzles.

Memory with Snowdrops and Waiting

for E, M, K, C

A whole hill fuzzy with the suspended heads
of snowdrops surprised you on a late-winter walk.
Unfocused, popping into view around a bend
in the trail, their pleated petals shook in the warm
breeze lifting from the south, little white buds
bobbing on their soft green stems

like a newborn's
head feeling its way around the slope of gravity,
the swivel of its spine. You wanted beyond want
to support a baby's neck, bundle and bale their fits,
feel the jump in your heart with each dip, each opened
dark eye on the blurry world that just bloomed.
You waited, and spent more time waiting to adopt
than those who swell in belly with anticipation.
Each day was a joy withheld, the loss of potential
familial energy: eyes, noses, ears, the distribution
of freckles

like the dotting of flowers in a thicket
you stumble into. Stunned and stirred, blood rush,
tender breast, *Galanthus*, milky blossom, the short
breath of being wholly changed by a flower
you didn't plant, that blooms for you anyway.

Tina Moessner

JOHN MOESSNER received his MFA from the University of Missouri-Kansas City. His poems have appeared in *New Letters*, *North American Review*, and *Poet Lore*. He lives in Kansas City.